Parenting
MADE EASY

This Book Will Change Your
Relationship with Your Child.

VIVIAN ELEBIYO-OKOJIE

PARENTING MADE EASY

This Book Will Change Your Relationship with Your Child.

Copyright © 2022 Vivian Elebiyo-Okojie

All rights reserved. No part of this book may be reproduced or transmitted in any form or by any means without the written permission of the author.

Scriptures marked KJV are taken from the KING JAMES VERSION (KJV): KING JAMES VERSION, public domain.

Scripture taken from the New King James Version®. Copyright © 1982 by Thomas Nelson. Used by permission. All rights reserved.

Published by:
Eleviv Publishing Group
Centerville, OH 45458
info@elevivpublishing.com
www.elevivpublishing.com

ISBN: 978-1-952744-61-7 PB
         978-1-952744-62-4 Ebook

Printed in the United States of America

Proverbs 22:6

Train up a child in the way he should go; even when he is old he will not depart from it.

Dedication

To my sons, Eric and Edward

May the world not ensnare and change who you are.

May the light that's within you shine like the stars.

May favor and peace be yours to find

May rejection and pain never reach you

May wisdom guide you when your mouth is talking

There is no better job or greater calling than being blessed to be called your mom.

I love you both.

-A Mother's Prayer

Table of *Content*

- *Dedication*
- *Introduction*
- **Growing Pains of Parenting** *13*
- **Becoming an Intentional Parent** *18*
- **How Intentional Parenting Changed my Life** *23*
- **How to be an Intentional Parent** *33*
- **Conclusion** *43*
- **100 Conversation Starters & Questions** *46*
- **Scriptures to Guide and Encourage you as a Parent** *55*
- **Prayers for the Children** *64*
- **Poems** *69*
- *About the author*

Introduction

Are you having hard conversations with your children? Are you teaching them the fundamentals? Are you equipping them with tools to navigate through life? Don't let culture, tradition, or the world dictate who they are and how to live.

My sons and I often have conversations about several topics, from gender expectations to taking responsibility, contentment, peer pressure, giving, societal expectations, gender roles, family, violence against women, etc.

It is crucial to start having these hard conversations. Start talking now. Please don't wait till they become teenagers.

So this past summer, we started something in my home that completely changed my life. We became intentional about communicating and connecting with our sons.

My husband and I started "Okojie's Conversations," we created a list of 100 questions and conversation starters and picked one daily to discuss with the boys. That was the best decision I've made as a parent and my most significant time investment since I birthed them.

The goal was simple, "TALK WITHOUT JUDGMENT, COMMUNICATE, AND CONNECT." We typically spend 30 minutes after bible study discussing each topic. We've talked about puberty, guns, dating, money, racism, tribalism, etc. The conversation starters aren't glossy, hiding from real issues. We talk about these things; we allow them to share their thoughts and provide some input, and that's it. Specific lessons are reiterated if needed, but I realized my sons became more comfortable and open. We can talk about almost anything now. Whereas they were hiding certain knowledge before, they can now express themselves better.

I'm thankful for the opportunity to do this with them. I'd gifted myself the most incredible joy by starting Okojies conversations. It was all I needed to navigate parenthood easily.

At the beginning of last school year, I'd gotten a call from my son's middle school principal. He had gotten into a verbal altercation with one of his teammates. We'd dropped him off early that day in school, and my sweet little boy had taunted his basketball teammate about how much of a better player he was than him. He went on to say not so many nice things. Ironically, my son had just started playing basketball two months prior, unlike some of his teammates.

Suddenly, he's able to make shots and becomes prideful, and not only that, he decides to pick on the one boy he felt he was better than. He hadn't learned how to use his words with grace and not to be puffed up. I was disappointed and angry. Having to explain to the principal that we raised him to be kind was something I hated doing. I made that situation about me; I yelled at him and took away his privileges. I never taught him the lessons I'd the opportunity to teach. After that first call, we had a few more calls from school. I soon realized that he constantly tried to prove something and speak his mind. Unfortunately, that got him lots of trouble.

Confidence is excellent, and delusional belief can transform your life because it births a high sense of self that others can't easily break. However, as a Christian, I also understand that everything I am and will be and all I have is given to me by God. Understanding how to use my words with grace and having self-confidence without taunting others or bringing them down was a lesson I had to teach him. This book discusses how my son's behavior made me feel.

I was angry at myself and very disappointed with him. I was inspired to write this book because of my experience and navigating the waters of parenting. Everything changed after we became intentional and the calls from school stopped. When raising children, you've got to understand that every child is different, so how you teach and lead them must also be different. This is not about you; it's bigger than you. It requires grace and being intentional.

Besides communicating with our boys, we intentionally connect with them and allow them to explore their gifts and talents. This encourages them to transmute their energies into passions that lift their spirit and make them a better version of themselves.

One thing that helped me was I had parents who allowed me to explore. I wasn't into sports, although I ran track in secondary school and was surrounded by adults who allowed me to expand my mind and explore my talents. My principal in secondary school was one of them, and several teachers along the way. Who pushed me and would speak words into my life that I see manifest.

I am intentional in helping my sons explore every passion. My first son loves basketball; he spent the entire summer practicing and honing his skills. We enrolled him in two basketball camps this summer and just found a personal coach. Having a child in sports is a lot of work and dedication. He also just signed up for Cross Country. My other son loves Beyblades and sometimes competes in tournaments across the state line.

When it comes to your children, be intentional, laser-focused, and tenaciously help them pursue their dreams and explore.

Allow your children to explore! Don't cage their talents or discourage them. I'm my kids' biggest hype man, supporting every dream or passion they have. I invest my time and energy into it and put all I've got into ensuring they succeed in whatever they do.

As I constantly encourage them to be the best in everything, I also give them room to change, grow, and fail.

I teach my sons to be vulnerable and share their emotions. We have to allow men to show all their feelings. They are trained not to be angry, cry, show weakness, and be a hard guy all the time. Telling men not to cry is unrealistic and sad. The fact a man can't share their pain without being laughed at or judged and called a sissy is sad. I allow my sons to be vulnerable with their emotions.

I'm raising my sons to show me how they feel and express their feelings. Stop saying boys don't cry. They should, and that's okay. Give them the space to express their feelings, ask them questions about how they feel, and allow them to vent and not bottle things up. Stop imposing on them burdens you can't carry. As a parent, focus on communicating, connecting, and allowing them to explore their talents and be in tune with their emotions.

Having well-rounded kids is essential and must be a priority. This book teaches parents about communicating, connecting, and exploring their children's interests. I hope this book helps as you journey through parenthood and make you a better parent.

Growing Pains of *Parenting*

My phone rang, and it was from my son's school; my heart skipped a beat; it was the middle school principal calling because my son had gotten into an argument with another boy. This call was the second phone call in three weeks. I drove to school, upset, fuming, and trying to find grace during the mess. Before that, we'd noticed inappropriate cuss words he used in conversations with friends online.

We had a rather challenging year with my 12-year-old, who had just started in a new private school in 6th grade. He got in trouble a few times for saying the wrong things or being late to a class period. His behavior during the second part of 6th grade broke my heart as a mom. He would be mean to his little brother or get in trouble for saying inappropriate things. We removed him from certain activities in school and told the principal to keep him away from some of the new boys who had just joined the school, and their influence on my son's behavior was becoming apparent and not what we wanted.

After that incident and the visit to the principal's office, we became even more concerned. We had so many questions: Why was our gentle little boy acting up? What happened to him? Was it a coming-of-age tantrum? Was I a bad mom? We just couldn't understand why he changed. His behavior and the possibility of getting suspended from school were even scarier.

I was overwhelmed with emotions and broken from his insistent behavior, which seemed to worsen. We tried everything: showing grace, getting angry, counseling, and punishing him. We just couldn't understand why our sweet little boy was changing before our eyes, and I felt helpless about how to help him. He was tired, too; I saw it, and he would be remorseful or unsure of what triggered his anger or his need to say those inappropriate things. When overcome by emotions, I would yell, threaten to take him back to Africa, and show him videos of little boys going to jail, but none of that helped.

    He is a terrific kid who can be easily influenced by others if not guided correctly. His need to prove himself in a new school was getting him in a lot of trouble, and he became an easy target for peer pressure or boys looking for sidekicks to get belligerent and silly. And because God's mark is on him, it's easy to pick him out of a group of other kids doing something wrong.

    We worried about our son and needed solutions, but nothing, not even my tears, helped the situation. I must admit I made it all about me and was over dramatic. At first, we considered homeschooling him since the new Christian Private school, which we thought would mold him in the Lord's way, was somehow changing our son. The school is fantastic because his brother attended the same school and never got in trouble, but somehow our eldest was finding it hard to adjust.

Nonetheless, we were proactive; we took away his privileges, stopped him from playing video games, deleted all social media accounts we noticed he opened without our knowledge, and held him accountable for every action. Temporary, it helped but not for long. There were still cracks in the walls. Somehow, we were still redirecting his behavior.

Finally, we've had enough; we had done all we could with our limited strength and started focusing on being more intentional. So, the first thing we focused on was PRAYER. My husband and I prayed and fasted over the issue, we also spent seven days fasting and praying, and he also joined in. We knew the devil was working overtime to change who he was and mess up the great destiny God had planned for him.

The prayers worked! But we had more work to do. We decided once school was out for the summer, we would start talking with him and his brother and having conversations with them. God wanted to work on his heart and help us focus on being intentional. Every child is different, and each child's parenting approach must be different. Suddenly it was apparent that God wanted more from us as parents. He wants us to be intentional and not waste opportunities to raise our sons right. I stopped the pity party and got to work. I blamed myself for being a lazy mom who thought shielding them away was a form of protection, but it wasn't. I thought protecting them would help me raise them right until I realized that that was an outdated way of parenting.

For so long, I was disillusioned and thought I was doing the right thing by shielding them away from shows or avoiding specific discussions. As a parent, I quickly realized that silence was never an option. Keeping my boys away from certain things was unrealistic and somewhat naive of me. I needed to talk with them to help them grow and be well-rounded. So, I began talking to him and being more intentional with my parenting approach, and everything changed.

Becoming an Intentional *Parent*

The journey to becoming an intentional parent was a decision borne out of the challenges with my son. It quickly became a gospel of some sort that I was ready to teach any parent who'd like to listen. Being an intentional parent is essential. You must have conversations with your child, spend time with them, and have fun with them. Parenting isn't a gamble or guesswork. You must be intentional about everything.

Unlike when we were growing up, certain things were unavailable, there was no internet, we didn't have cell phones, and we didn't have TV shows that explored inappropriate topics. I remember when we watched things on black and white television, and there was nothing to watch except a few shows and the news. There was no reality TV, YouTube, Google, Tik Tok, Facebook, or Instagram. There weren't magazines telling us to look one way or think another way to be liked or desirable. But this generation is exposed to so much information, thanks to the internet.

We are in the information gateway period where information is accessible to anyone and everyone, so that means even the child in the village, the child on the street who doesn't even have food to eat, has access to some level of information. Because that access is available, it'll be silly for a parent to think that their child or their children do not have access to inappropriate things, and even if they don't have the internet, they listen to their peers in school.

So, creating a time to have conversations with my sons was just what I needed. It was a time to share my heart with my sons and hear them. They also share their heart with me, their thoughts and feelings about a situation or scenario. It has awarded me just that "Peace of Mind" I needed as a parent. I get to know what my boys think about specific issues. It's a very non-judgmental way of getting to grow as a family. I realized quickly that shielding this information and acting like those things don't exist is not the way to grow as a family.

 Becoming intentional means guiding your children's choices in everything, from sports to career choices, behavior, and life choices. It means asking questions about what they like and don't like and encouraging them to be more intentional about setting goals.

 My 12 years old loves basketball and being physically fit; he also has a knack for music especially playing instruments, so we signed him for the band and bought him a keyboard and a clarinet. We signed him up at the YMCA for basketball, and he also plays for the school. This year he joins OSHAA for Cross Country. Nurturing their gifts and talents is very important in becoming more intentional. It means investing time and resources into building those skills. The Williams sisters, Serena and Venus, were pushed by their father to become the best tennis players, but it didn't happen overnight.

The Jacksons were nurtured in music to become the best.

There are many examples of children whose parents invested time and resources into building and encouraging their children in sports, entertainment, education, skills, talents, etc. These things don't just happen overnight. You must encourage them to pursue those things and be ready to support them. You can't shove an idea on them and try to project the life you want on them; you must prayerfully watch them and see what they enjoy doing. One of my nieces has an ear for language, so I encouraged the mom to sign her up for Spanish classes. My youngest son loves computers and building, so this summer, we focused on coding classes and software he can get acquainted with to learn design and game coding.

Remember that a child's desires may change a million times but be available to guide them. We are all created for a purpose, and we all have something we are meant to contribute to the world. Encourage your children to explore new skills and opportunities; don't talk them out of their dreams or passions. Engage them in a way that allows them to grow. Watch them keenly like a hawk. Don't waste your time and money on placing them in extracurricular activities they can't stand. One of my sons hates ice skating but loves swimming; he did it for a few weeks, and we never bothered signing up anymore.

    Becoming an intentional parent requires action on how you plan to raise your children. You want well-rounded children who are book smart and life learners who explore and express themselves in ways that drive their passion and point to purpose.

How Intentional Parenting Changed *my Life*

I'm a Christian and would refer to the Bible. When I think about the story of Eli when Elis' sons were misbehaving, he turned a blind eye, and even when people told him his children were messing up, he acted like he didn't know; at the end of the day, that costs him his life, it costs him his ministry, and it costs him everything. When the principal would call and complain about my son, I would listen, ask questions, thank him for contacting us, and scold him once we got home. If I ever felt he was falsely accused, I would also address it in an email.

Neglecting the children and expecting them to raise themselves is a costly mistake. Turning a blind eye to your children is equally as bad. The moment we became more intentional, it was clear we'd been doing things wrong. We weren't bad parents; we were far from it. However, our approach needed to be reconsidered and reworked. I was having a conversation with one of my sisters about intentional parenting. I told her of a time I used to hide certain commercials from the boys; I would quickly switch the channel. Sadly, I can't be with my boys 24/7; they have devices, go to school, hang out with friends, etc.

Indeed, there are things you must shield them away from, but unfortunately, you can't protect them from everything. It's an echelon task and unrealistic. There's so much you can do as a parent because even when you're not there, do they know what you think? Do they understand how you feel about a particular issue?

Until we started "Okojie's Conversations," I was like a duck waddling in the lake. These questions I created were a guide to help me navigate the treacherous waters of parenting. It gave me the tools needed to know them more and be more intentional about what I want my boys to know.

Suddenly, things began to change. We talked more, we laughed more, and we were no longer getting calls from school. I also realized both boys became much more open. It was also a time that helped us gather, talk, and learn. It wasn't a time to yell out rules. We were not saying, "don't do this; we were asking them questions and what they thought about it. Then we shared our thoughts, what our family stood for, and what our faith demands.

We typically end the conversation with a plea and say this is what we would appreciate you doing. All of this is done with grace, keeping the word of God in our hearts. It isn't the time to shove your belief down their throat because you would mess things up. They would not even want to continue the conversation. You also can't demand your way or start scolding or questioning their belief; there will be plenty of time for that. For instance, if your child's belief about smoking is outside of your family values or faith, listen to her, share your thoughts from a physical or science-based standpoint and let it be. Wait a week or so, then look for teachable moments to speak on it again. The worst thing you can do during a conversation is to make it about you and your belief.

In my family, we talk about everything from bullying to alcohol to smoking to drugs, suicide, and depression. We've talked about guns, what they think about the issue, and not necessarily what mommy or daddy thinks; it's more like, I know you're aware of this issue, what are your thoughts? We listen, and it's remarkable when they share their thoughts, and because we're not judgmental, it helps us gather information on how to guide them and understand them better. This single decision has helped us understand our boys better. I honestly believe that everything becomes more straightforward when a parent invests that time to get to know their child individually.

You are not just throwing rules and regulations out there; you are simply saying, I want to learn how to raise you; I want to know your thoughts, what you think, and how you feel. Having these conversations is essential; trust me, you don't want to throw them out into this world and expect them to know or understand what you think about certain situations.

You want to lay a good foundation, not just by saying don't do this or don't do that. Our parents did that; my mom told me if a guy touched me, I would get pregnant, which freaked me out even in college. I would freak out when a guy kissed me or when a guy hugged me. I later found out that sex was much more than just the birds and the bees. It's so much more than that, so like many others, I had to learn on my own.

Your primary job as a parent is to have a conversation with your child, and I kid you not; this was the best thing I did for my family this year beyond everything else that I've accomplished this year; this was by far my greatest joy.

Typically, we have Bible study and then have conversations afterward; we pick a topic, talk about it, get their response, then share our thoughts. If there's a need for any biblical information to bolster our point, we share it as well. As a Christian, it's easy always to throw God into everything and neglect our responsibilities. Sometimes we miss the point we are trying to make by over-spiritualizing everything. For this to be effective, you must share your thoughts as a parent, what you think about the topic, and your family values. Do you have a principle for your family, what is your family ethos, and what is your family's vision and mission?

Governments, entertainment industries, and organizations are working hard on pushing ungodly agendas and propagating evil doctrines to indoctrinate children into lifestyles or behaviors that are against biblical values. We've got to be careful and be ready to train our children; the Bible says to train your child in the way he should go, and when he is old, he will not depart from it. My goal with this book is to encourage parents to pursue that time to communicate, connect, instruct and equip their children. Don't wait until they are in college and they've already created a map for their lives. You've got to start young; if you have teenagers talk to them, you can still have these conversations even if you have college-aged children. It's never too late to be intentional.

I have a 10-year-old and a 12-year-old; I started being more intentional this year. But you could start having this conversation as early as a child is at a knowing age. A four-year-old can have certain conversations, but what you would say to a four-year-old would be utterly different from the conversation you would have with a 10-year-old or even a teenager. You can even have this conversation with your college-age child or just simple conversations as a family, no matter the age. Again, every family is different, and each child's maturity level is different.

There are six points to remember if you will use this guide.

- Do not be judgmental.
- Create a time that works for everyone so that you can have this conversation without distraction
- Listen, don't just speak and throw out do's and don'ts. This manual is not a "don't do this" or "don't do that" manual. This manual is a great way to have conversations as a family. You will get to know each other better, so I encourage you not to spend the entire time talking to them without listening. Do not make this about yourself.

You're not a professor trying to say here is a lesson plan and throw everything on them. You are saying this is my thought. I want to know what your thoughts are.
- Always let the children go first; you could talk about the issue briefly, but let them speak, and then you add your thoughts, the family stance, or what your faith believes.
- You could always add other questions; this is not an exhaustive list, so you can add and take out questions as needed. You can omit questions that you are not comfortable with at that particular time or if it's not age-appropriate but do not skip anything just because you're afraid or you're worried, or you're not sure your child is aware. Certain things aren't age-appropriate; for instance, I won't talk about puberty to a 2-year-old or a four-year-old, but I'll talk about bullying and peer pressure, friendship, happiness, love, sharing, etc.
- Pray! Pray before you have a conversation; pray after you have a conversation.

Always look for teachable moments when watching a movie, news, or when a commercial comes on. You can find teachable moments during a ride to practice, from school, at dinner, or at home. You could also set up a special moment to talk like we do after Bible study. Make it simple, don't make it too long either. Conversations should not be more than 10 to 20 minutes only. If it gets exciting, then you can go with the flow. Don't just keep talking; it becomes weird, especially if it's a topic like puberty or sex or strange topics that kids don't necessarily want to discuss.

When talking to them, although I have boys, I speak to them about issues women deal with as well. We've talked about menstruation because I've noticed that many men grow up, start dating, get married, and are clueless about what women deal with biologically. You could have conversations that are not just gender-based but general conversations that could help your child understand how to relate with someone of the opposite sex.

Be open, read the room, understand your child's age and maturity level, and then have the appropriate conversations. Beyond that, have fun. It's been fun for me; sometimes, I tease them about specific topics I want to discuss. We're still trying to do the puberty topic, and it's been a bit dicey. But I hope you will enjoy this as much as I have; I hope it changes the dynamics of your family for the better. Again, be ready to listen because this book is not for you if you cannot actively listen to your child and be non-judgmental about the conversations you will be having. If you can't but judge, then this book is not for you. Maybe you need time to sort out certain things in your life, and perhaps you need time to grow as a parent.

    Be ready to listen and slow to speak, and if you're that parent who would yell and scream or go crazy, then maybe this book is not for you. Still, if you are that parent who is ready to learn, who is prepared to listen, and teach, then this book will change your life and the life of your children, and more than that, it will make parenting simple and easy for you.

How to be a More Intentional *Parent*

The Bible is filled with terrible parenting examples, parents who turned a blind eye to their children's misbehavior. Our mandate as parents is to teach and train our children; that's our primary assignment.

Being an intentional parent means making conscious efforts to make informed parenting choices. It means finding time to connect with your child and yourself. Being intentional means being deliberate about your choices and actions as a parent and laying down the proper foundation for your children. Be intentional about how you raise your child, from spending time with them, having conversations, and letting them know how much you love them.

As mentioned earlier, the authoritarian parenting style or being an overprotective parent isn't always helpful in raising children. When you are intentional, you can guide their choices. They understand that your guide comes from a place of love, and it's easier for them to accept.

So how can you be a more intentional parent?

- Allow them to participate in family decisions and decisions that have to do with their lives and future. Tell them about new changes in the family; you are buying a new house, let them be fully aware, you want to change their school, let them know.
- Communicate with your children (about everything and anything): Keep in mind the things you discuss, and keep in mind the age and maturity level of the child.
- Encourage them to express their opinions respectfully. Let them talk, don't shut them up, don't say, "you talk too much," and all of them express themselves. Allow them to show varied emotions of hurt, joy, excitement, confusion, anger, etc. Don't

ignore their feelings or downplay them. Let them own their EVERY feeling and process their feelings safely.
- Listen to their point of view. Your child(ren) are humans and have a right to self-express and share their opinions about ANYTHING. So, don't tell your child, "You are just a child" hear them out and use that as teachable moments if need be.
- Give your children age-appropriate chores. Research has found that giving your kid chores may have long-lasting benefits academically, socially, emotionally, and professionally.
- Expose them to luxury. Kids exposed to luxury would not settle for less; they become familiar with luxury. They also won't be tricked by it, and luxury won't be weaponized to steal their innocence. Get them used to art, fine cuisine, travel, and progressive thinking and lifestyle. It doesn't have to break the bank, either. I would cook and serve them healthy gourmet-style meals, take them to museums, and much more.

- Give your children the freedom to make age-appropriate decisions. It means giving them the autonomy to decide what to do. You have nothing to worry about once you give them the necessary tools.
- Spend time with them, go out, travel, and do fun things with your child. Have FUN, don't just be their parent, be their friend. Get ice cream, dance, cook, have pillow fights, tickle them, have a fun handshake, etc. I have a goofy handshake with my son, I don't get it, but I love it. I talk about Beyblades with my youngest son; I don't get it, but I enjoy how his eyes lit up whenever he talks about the different gimmicks.
- Let your child be bored. Provide less structured learning environments where children can use their imagination to entertain themselves. Remove the TV, phones, and computers sometimes and allow them to explore and be bored enough to create or look for ways to distract themselves.
- Create a date time with your children. I

take my boys out and encourage their dad to do the same. I would take them out together or individually. It's that time with just Mommy or that memorable ride to the store with daddy. My friend has special days with her daughter; another has a date night with her daughters for their birthdays. A friend promised all her children a trip to any county in the world after graduating high school. We have Friday movie night at the Okojie's residence, and the boys enjoy it. Find time to take them out for ice cream, to the park, to the movies, or on a trip.

- Expose them to much-needed time they will remember as they grow older. Be intentional about it.
- If you have more than one child, have specific days for each child to get to know them better. Kids get excited about having their OWN time with mom or dad.
- Grab little pieces of time to connect – when shopping, driving in the car, waiting in the queue, etc.
- Start a monthly outing routine or weekly

routine to connect with them. Simple things like going to the park and the mall would mean a lot.
- Create a mission, vision, and ethos for your family and children. Being intentional means setting goals and having an overall vision for your family.

Intentional parenting means having a plan and prioritizing where you put your time and energy. Those priorities then guide your day-to-day decision-making and what commitments you make. As an intentional parent, every decision must have the children in mind, from what job to take, where to travel, what community to build a home, etc. As a parent, you make many decisions daily in the interest of your children. I was discussing with a friend how life is so short and our time with our children is limited and must be cherished.

We must be thankful for God's gift to impact their lives and know our everyday decisions will directly shape their lives. In the book of Deuteronomy 6:7-9, Moses wanted the Israelites to the next generation the truth of God's wisdom. *"Write these commandments that I've given you today on your hearts. Get them inside of you, and then get them inside your children. Talk about them wherever you are, sitting at home or walking in the street; talk about them from the time you get up in the morning to when you fall into bed at night. Tie them on your hands and foreheads as a reminder; inscribe them on the doorposts of your homes and on your city gates."*

Intentional parenting is a mandate and a blessing to pass down knowledge, show them love, and for us, not see parenting as a burden. Being an intentional parent means paying attention to your children, listening to them, and learning how to serve them better. This deliberate action requires us to quiet distractions, especially from social media, cell phones, and TV. It means we are willing to learn, say sorry when we mess up, and seek out help in areas we are ineffective.

The number one aspect of intentionality is COMMUNICATING AND CONNECTING. The other element of intentionality is INSTRUCTING AND EQUIPPING.

COMMUNICATION, CONNECTION, AND INSTRUCTION HELP WITH INTENTIONAL PARENTING

- You must be instructional and persistent in communicating with your children. What do I want my child to know for their next developmental stage? What do I want them to learn? Equip them with the tools to navigate life, relationships, and more. Prepare your children for the world by equipping them with the skills necessary to succeed and cope with failures. But beyond the life lessons and education, we must exemplify traits and model behaviors we want to see our children emulate
- Learn to communicate better and more clearly and be a good listener.
- Constantly teach them and always make your home a place to learn.
- Children love learning, so be available and intentional about teaching them. Look for teachable moments daily to reinforce previous lessons and teach new things.
- Encourage Independence and Problem

Solving: Being an intentional parent means raising independent thinkers and problem solvers. Give them the tools to navigate the world and trust their judgment in making the right choices; this would help them view the world differently and be better equipped to understand the world. Encourage them to think critically about decisions instead of doing everything for them.
- Connect with your children. Play with them, play hide and seek, jump around, tap into your inner child and express it freely.
- Work on not yelling at your children and overcome parenting frustrations. Bursting out in anger isn't always the most effective way of communicating our frustrations. Eventually, your child would tune you out, and you'd lose the opportunity to communicate with them effectively.
- Curb entitlement by teaching children about money. These lessons must start very early. Let them understand that if they want anything in life, they must work

for it.
- Implement consequences because it facilitates emotional learning & well-being. Make sure they learn lessons when they are wrong and don't just gloss over issues or wrongdoings. They must understand that every action calls for a reaction.
- Connect with them daily and as often as you can. The time we have to impact our children's lives is limited, and it is essential not to take it for granted.
- Be clear on your goals for the family but be flexible for changes. If you've equipped your son to play the violin and after ten lessons and $600, he decides he wants to play the clarinet, be open to changes but be firm on consequences if he makes quitting a habit.
- Above all, find time for yourself, equip yourself, take care of yourself, grow mentally, and let God lead you.

Conclusion

So, on a final note, this book has a list of 100 questions and comes with a journal to fill out your child's responses and a place to share your thoughts. I also created a journal for the children to share their thoughts about the questions. This book, included with the journal, would help you create unforgettable moments with your children. You will have funny moments and some sad moments as well. All in all, you get to understand one another, which is the most important thing.

Do not rush through it; set the pace that works for your family. Don't be in a hurry to answer every question, linger on a topic for weeks if you have to. The most important thing is creating that time to talk to and understand your child(ren).

I want to encourage you to take this very seriously. As I mentioned at the beginning of the book, this changed my life, my parenting style, and the level of comfort, I would say, around specific issues. I felt it brought me closer to my kids, and I pray they feel the same way. I think I'm more comfortable talking about uncomfortable issues, and they are more comfortable sharing certain matters and talking about certain things. They are no longer hiding because I think when you see the heart of someone and you know their thoughts, everything becomes simple, and no one is hiding.

Conversations set a foundation you can quickly build upon, which helps the relationship flourish and parenting easy. The 100 questions are just sample questions you can ask, and it's simply a guideline; you could always add more questions or remove things that don't fit your family.

I also encourage you to have follow-up questions; you could prepare a day before; this would help prepare your mind. You could also read up more on it, especially if it's a subject you are unfamiliar with, and pray for the grace to listen and not judge. Also, for the grace to hear their hearts without being judgmental. I hope you can be an active listener and not miss the opportunity to get to know them better. It isn't the time to yell at them or raise your nose at their beliefs; it's a time to impart knowledge and hear their thoughts.

For every question, be attentive; you can also give scenarios and ask follow-up questions. No matter what your child(ren) says, make sure you listen, give your thoughts, and share your family values and principles on the topic; you can also share what your faith says about the issue. I created these conversations to help you get closer to your child. You want to lay a good foundation and create a safe space for the children, not a space where they are scared because they don't know what you as a parent think. Note that some questions are not one-off; you must constantly reinforce, create teachable moments, revisit the questions or responses, and talk in-depth as needed.

100 Conversation Starters and

1. Let's talk about puberty.
2. What are your thoughts on bullying? *(Joshua 1:9, Ephesians 4:32, Luke 6:31)*
3. Let's talk about body image. Does it matter how big or little you are?
4. Do you think smoking is okay?
5. What are your thoughts on drugs?
6. What are your thoughts on guns and shooting in school?
7. What are your thoughts on education and its importance?
8. What are your thoughts on slavery, sexism, tribalism, colorism, and racism? *(Matthew 22:39)*
9. Does skin color matter?

10. What are your thoughts on obeying the law, authority, police brutality, etc.?
11. What are your thoughts on respect for women? Respect for Men?
12. What are your thoughts on emotional intelligence and how we treat others and handle situations? *(Ephesians 4:32)*
13. Is it okay to be delusional about your abilities or have a high sense of self? *(Proverbs 3:5)*
14. How we see ourselves matters; what do you think of yourself?
15. Are friendships and relationships important? Should they define our lives?
16. Is success essential, and is it the same as wealth?
17. What are your thoughts on nepotism?
18. Do you ever feel unloved or unheard? When or how?
19. Is physical fitness and activities important?
20. What are your thoughts on taking care of yourself?
21. How important is nutrition to you and eating?

22. How do you feel when you know someone likes you? Or don't like you?
23. How do you feel when you know you are being heard?
24. How do you feel when you are recognized for something good?
25. What do you want to be when you grow up?
26. What would you love to do with your children when you become a dad or mom?
27. Would you want to get married? Why or why not?
28. Would you want to have children? Why or why not? (James 1:17)
29. What is a good age to start dating?
30. What do you know about sex? What is a good age to start having sex?
31. What are your thoughts on people influencing your choices negatively?
32. What is self-esteem?
33. How do you show respect to yourself, others, and authority?
34. How do you set boundaries?
35. What does cleanliness mean and care for

our world and environment?
36. What do you think the role of a mom or wife is?
37. What do you think the role of a dad or husband is?
38. What do you think the role of man and woman is?
39. What are your thoughts on peer pressure?
40. What do you enjoy doing the most?
41. What do you always want to do?
42. If you can be anything, what would you want to be?
43. What are your thoughts on asking for help?
44. What are your thoughts on sharing your time, money, and resources?
45. What are your thoughts on depending on others?
46. What do you think love is?
47. What are your thoughts on violence and gangs, and cliques?
48. What are your thoughts on abortion?
49. What are your thoughts on lying and honesty? What are your thoughts on lying

to get out of trouble or to get ahead?
50. What are your thoughts on honest living and doing what you can to be comfortable?
51. What are your thoughts on mental health and its importance?
52. What are your thoughts on depression?
53. What are your thoughts on suicide?
54. What are your thoughts on drinking alcohol, smoking, or vaping?
55. Is beating or hitting a (wo)man okay?
56. What are your thoughts on helping a spouse around the house?
57. What are your thoughts on abstinence?
58. When you notice injustice, what do you do?
59. When dating, is it your responsibility to take care of the girl/boy?
60. When dating, is it a man's responsibility to take care of you?
61. Is it okay for men to cry?
62. What are your thoughts on homosexuality and LGBTQ?
63. Do you believe God is real? Heaven? Hell? *(Psalm145:9, Proverbs 30:5,*

Deuteronomy 5:29)
64. Do you believe we all serve the same God?
65. Is it okay to be friends with people who don't have the same faith as you?
66. Is it okay to be silent when you see people doing something wrong?
67. No means no! What does that mean? When a girl says no, it means no. Explain what rape is.
68. Talk about wrong and right touches.
69. What are your thoughts on guarding your heart?
70. What are your thoughts on setting priorities?
71. What are your thoughts on setting goals?
72. What would you do if someone told you to do something terrible?
73. What would you do if someone online asked for your home address or pictures?
74. What should you do if you are online and someone asks for your naked pictures or shares weird images with you?
75. What should you do if someone tells you to sneak out of the house without your

parent's approval? *(Colossians 3:20)*
76. What are your thoughts on giving? *(James 1:27)*
77. What are your thoughts on working?
78. What are your thoughts on financial responsibility? Debt, credit, investing, saving, liability, credit scores?
79. What are your thoughts on death and dying?
80. What are your thoughts on material possession and simple or extravagant living? *(Colossians 3:2)*
81. What makes you sad? What should you do when someone is unhappy?
82. What makes you happy? Are you happy?
83. What makes you angry? What can I do as a parent when you are angry?
84. What makes you sad?
85. What irritates you?
86. What activities overwhelm you and make you unhappy?
87. How are you a good citizen of the earth?
88. What new things do you think will make you happy?
89. What would you like to learn?

90. On a scale of 1-10, how am I doing as a parent?
91. What can I do to be a better parent?
92. What can you do to be a better child? *(Colossians 3:20)*
93. On a scale of 1-10, how do you think you are doing as a child?
94. What are your thoughts on entitlement? Does anyone owe you anything? Do you owe anyone anything?
95. Who contributes to your happiness or unhappiness? Does your family, sibling, friends, teachers, and trainers make you happy or sad?
96. What contributes to your happiness or unhappiness? Does your school, afterschool programs, camp, hobby, sports, and church, make you happy or sad?
97. If you can learn anything, what would it be?
98. Is it okay to tell people everything about you?
99. What do you need beyond the basics that we provide?

100. Do you think the discipline and consequences in our family are fair? Would you change anything? Why?

Scriptures to Guide and Encourage you as a

1. *James 1:27* – "Religion that is pure and undefiled before God the Father is this: to visit orphans and widows in their affliction, and to keep oneself unstained from the world."

2. *Psalm 145:9* – "The LORD is good to all, and his mercy is over all that he has made."

3. *Joshua 1:9* – "Have I not commanded you? Be strong and courageous. Do not be frightened, and do not be dismayed, for the LORD your God is with you wherever you go."

4. *Philippians 4:4* – "Rejoice in the Lord always; again I will say, rejoice!"

5. Matthew 22:39 – "And a second is like it: You

shall love your neighbor as yourself."

6. **Numbers 6:24** – "The LORD bless you and keep you."

7. **Colossians 3:2** – "Set your minds on things that are above, not on things that are on earth."

8. **Colossians 3:16** – "Let the word of Christ dwell in you richly, teaching and admonishing one another in all wisdom, singing psalms and hymns and spiritual songs, with thankfulness in your hearts to God."

9. **1 John 5:3** – "For this is the love of God, that we keep his commandments. And his commandments are not burdensome."

10. **Proverbs 30:5** – "Every word of God proves true; he is a shield to those who take refuge in him."

11. **Hebrews 13:8** – "Jesus Christ is the same yesterday, today and forever."

12. **Psalm 150:6** – "Let everything that has breath praise the LORD! Praise the LORD!"

13. *Proverbs 3:5* – "Trust in the LORD with all your heart, and do not lean on your own understanding."

14. *Romans 10:13* – "For 'everyone who calls on the name of the Lord will be saved.'"

15. *Romans 3:23* – "For all have sinned and fall short of the glory of God."

16. *Matthew 5:14* – "You are the light of the world. A city set on a hill cannot be hidden."

17. *Psalm 139:14* – "I praise you, for I am fearfully and wonderfully made. Wonderful are your works; my soul knows it very well."

18. *Colossians 3:20* – "Children, obey your parents in everything, for this pleases the Lord."

19. *James 1:17* – "Every good gift and every perfect gift is from above, coming down from the Father of lights, with whom there is no variation or shadow due to change."

20. *1 John 1:5* – "This is the message we have heard from him and proclaim to you, that God

is light, and in him is no darkness at all."

21. *Ephesians 4:32* – "Be kind to one another, tenderhearted, forgiving one another, as God in Christ forgave you."

22. *1 John 3:23* – "And this is his commandment, that we believe in the name of his Son Jesus Christ and love one another, just as he has commanded us."

23. *Psalm 56:3* – "When I am afraid, I put my trust in you."

24. *Psalm 118:24* – "This is the day that the LORD has made; let us rejoice and be glad in it."

25. *Psalm 119:105* – "Your word is a lamp to my feet and a light to my path."

26. *Psalm 136:1* – "Give thanks to the LORD, for he is good, for his steadfast love endures forever."

27. *Luke 6:31* – "And as you wish that others would do to you, do so to them."

28. *Philippians 4:13* – "I can do all things through

him who strengthens me."

29. **Psalm 138:1** – "I give you thanks, O LORD, with my whole heart; before the gods I sing your praise."

30. **Isaiah 30:15** – "For thus said the Lord GOD, the Holy One of Israel, 'In returning and rest you shall be saved; in quietness and in trust shall be your strength.'"

31. **Proverbs 22:6** -"Start children off on the way they should go, and even when they are old they will not turn from it."

32. **Isaiah 49:15-16** - "Can a mother forget the baby at her breast and have no compassion on the child she has borne? Though she may forget, I will not forget you! See, I have engraved you on the palms of my hands; your walls are ever before me. "

33. **Hebrews 12:11** - "No discipline seems pleasant at the time, but painful. Later on, however, it produces a harvest of righteousness and peace for those who have been trained by

it."

34. *Ephesians 6:4* - "Fathers, do not exasperate your children; instead, bring them up in the training and instruction of the Lord."

35. *Proverbs 17:6* - "Children's children are a crown to the aged, and parents are the pride of their children."

36. *1 John 5:21* - "Dear children, keep yourselves from idols."

37. *Ephesians 5:1* - "Follow God's example, therefore, as dearly loved children."

38. *Matthew 5:9* - "Blessed are the peacemakers, for they will be called children of God."

39. *Acts 16:31* - "They replied, "Believe in the Lord Jesus, and you will be saved—you and your household."

40. *Galatians 3:26-27* - "So in Christ Jesus you are all children of God through faith, for all of you who were baptized into Christ have clothed yourselves with Christ."

41. *3 John 1:4* - "I have no greater joy than to hear that my children are walking in the truth."

42. *Proverbs 15:5* - "A fool spurns a parent's discipline, but whoever heeds correction shows prudence."

43. *Romans 8:14* - "For those who are led by the Spirit of God are the children of God."

44. *1 John 3:1* - See what great love the Father has lavished on us, that we should be called children of God! And that is what we are! The reason the world does not know us is that it did not know him."

45. *1 Timothy 5:8* - "Anyone who does not provide for their relatives, and especially for their own household, has denied the faith and is worse than an unbeliever."

46. *John 1:12* - "Yet to all who did receive him, to those who believed in his name, he gave the right to become children of God."

47. *Romans 8:19* - "For the creation waits in eager expectation for the children of God to be

revealed."

48. *1 John 3:2-3* - "Dear friends, now we are children of God, and what we will be has not yet been made known. But we know that when Christ appears, we shall be like him, for we shall see him as he is. All who have this hope in him purify themselves, just as he is pure."

49. *Romans 8:16* - "The Spirit himself testifies with our spirit that we are God's children."

50. *Romans 8:15* - "The Spirit you received does not make you slaves, so that you live in fear again; rather, the Spirit you received brought about your adoption to sonship. And by him we cry, "Abba, Father."

51. *Deuteronomy 5:29* - "Oh, that their hearts would be inclined to fear me and keep all my commands always, so that it might go well with them and their children forever!"

52. *Deuteronomy 4:40* - "Keep his decrees and commands, which I am giving you today, so that it may go well with you and your children after

you and that you may live long in the land the Lord your God gives you for all time."

53. *Ephesians 5:8* - "For you were once darkness, but now you are light in the Lord. Live as children of light."

Prayers for the

1. Lord, I pray that the Lord guide and protect my children.
2. May they love themselves and others.
3. May the world not change them or destroy the great destiny God has for them.
4. May integrity guide their hearts
5. May peace, love, and God's favor be theirs.
6. May my children live and not die.
7. May sickness or terminal illness stay far from my children.
8. May life be kind to them, and may life be good to them.
9. May life be easy and not hard for my children.
10. May my children be blessed of the Lord.

11. May my children give me peace.
12. My children will never suffer.
13. Where I never got to professionally, financially, and in life, my children will surpass me.
14. My children will be a blessing to their generation.
15. My children will change the world for good.
16. My children will find their purpose.
17. The devil will not thwart my children's destiny.
18. They will not be trapped, deceived, or mistreated.
19. My children shall be for signs and wonders.
20. They will not be victims of someone else's mistake, hate, racism, prejudice, or sick and twisted desires.
21. May depression, anxiety, or any mental illness stay away from my children and home.
22. May my children always find joy in everything.
23. May my children not be victims of school shootings, stray bullets, or accidents.
24. May my children not be victims of bullying

and torture.
25. My children will not go to jail or be in trouble with the law.
26. I will not lose my children to the devices of the devil.
27. I will not lose my children to suicide.
28. May their life be a point of positive inspiration for others.
29. May they succeed in life and live a wealthy and healthy life.
30. May they know God and serve Him all the days of their lives.
31. May they never fall or fail.
32. I will live long to witness all the amazing things God will do in their lives.
33. May their mouths be filled with kind words all the days of their lives.
34. (Mention your children's name) your lives will not be hard.
35. You will not be a victim of peer pressure.
36. You will be a leader and not a follower.
37. You will be the head and not the tail.
38. You will be above and not beneath.
39. The Lord will guide you and keep you.
40. Your steps are ordered by God now and

always.
41. You will not be entangled by the world.
42. You will find love at the right time and have a blessed life.
43. May you never be taken advantage of, used, or mistreated.
44. May you not be physically, emotionally, mentally, spiritually, or sexually abused.
45. May you not be molested. Pedophiles will not see you or come near you.
46. I cancel every spirit of suicide and self-harming spirits and behaviors.
47. May wisdom guide your lips.
48. May honesty, kindness, and love be your guide.
49. May your barns always be filled with goodly things.
50. May happiness never elude you, and may you be happy all the days of your life.
51. You will not die young; I will see your children's children.
52. May you not wander the earth confused or unsure.
53. May you not bring shame to yourself or the family.

54. May you be the best in everything you do.
55. May your heart always be filled with love towards others.
56. May you be useful to yourself and your generation.
57. May evil stay far from you.
58. May you not beg or borrow.
59. May you not be a liar or thief.
60. I command every organ in your body to work well and not break down.
61. May you be favored all the days of your life.
62. May you always find reasons to dance and live life.
63. May your mountains always look small and God's grace big enough.
64. May the Lord guide and teach me how to love and raise you.
65. May I learn how to connect and communicate with you, using the word of the Lord as my guide.

Poem

Dear God

I hope my sons never know what a goodbye kiss feels like.
I hope love is true, is transparent, it stays!
I hope it's filled with thousands of butterflies.
Filled with God, filled with peace and forgiveness
Not vileness of fleshly desires that evaporate in darkness. I pray integrity guides them, truth shields them, and kindness be their anchor.

Dear God

I pray this for my adopted daughter as well. That a man will find her desirable enough to wait for her

Tell truths to her, not lie to her
I hope love doesn't leave her with scars
nor leave her bruised or battered
I pray it leaves her with songs blazing in her heart
I pray love doesn't just hang out temporarily but for a lifetime
That she only sheds sweet tears not of pain or suffering but of hearts rapturing

Dear God
I pray as a mom; I can teach my children how to love, be wise, be kind
I remember the breaks in my fragile heart. The innocence of love unfeigned
Help me to teach them how I stared into the eyes of the opposition and won
How I fought lions of hate and broke the jaws of lust
How I found love, gave love, and through it, birth love.

Dear God
I pray that my children's father braze the cold of temptation and embrace life, his life, the

one wrapped in love.
A life not wrapped in the worries of life and truly walk in his calling as a father.
A life not intertwined by the limbs of falsehood, a daughter of the devil with warped lips
Be a reason for our children to call on God, to serve Him.
Be the man that most men yawn to be
Let his seeds praise him. Let the ones from his loins I brought forth be enchanted by his strength. Let them learn about integrity, imprinted in his steps and discipline and hardwork in his palms.
Let him be wrapped fully in us, as we are the glue to his beautiful life.

Dear God
I pray my children's grandparents get to live long to see the legacy of truth and hard work
To see the reward of what simplicity can bring
To see what prayers can do
To see the miracle in imperfection
Their lives might not be chiseled by the

western standards
Marriages that stood the test of time
In remembrance, that love comes in stages and might not be an all-you-can-eat buffet.
That patience is the key to life.
Material gains and collections of accolades do not measure that success
But it is measured by how you have lived and given yourself in bits
That it is possible to live with 20 other relatives, and mom goes to bed hungry but never angry by the hand she's been dealt.
That love may not come with "I love you" every morning, and hearts might be separated by beds cornered in different rooms.
Nevertheless, the love stands in the fountain of youth they both drink from, love lines written in wrinkles till death comes.
Till the last breath
Till those arms that tilled the ground and walked the streets of life wither because it's finally time to rest and let their seed carry on the royal bloodline, but until then, I pray my children continue to pay their respect to

the man and woman who decided to give mommy a chance.

About the Author

Vivian Elebiyo-Okojie is an entrepreneur, youth minister, and founder of Bread of Hope, an organization she started in 2022 after a clarion call on January 30th, 2022, to purchase 100 acres of land in Ibadan, Nigeria, to build a City of Hope, a center of a restoration, and space for equipping the younger generation. She runs a publishing company and global marketplace for authors with an uncanny passion for artistic expressions through words and more.

Vivian shares her faith talks about family and her non-profit work, and sometimes shares food recipes through her online platforms and on God, Love, and Jollof, an online faith-sharing community and podcast. Vivian is a powerful and engaging speaker and has spoken at numerous events, including Praire View University, TBN, Department of Health Florida, InnovateHER, HCC, Churches, Schools, several radio stations, and events around the world.

She has appeared in top media outlets worldwide.

Find out more about Bread of Hope by visiting breadhopelife.org and more about her ministry on social media and YouTube @ Godlovejollof

This book comes with a journal to help you stay committed on this journey.